I0439947

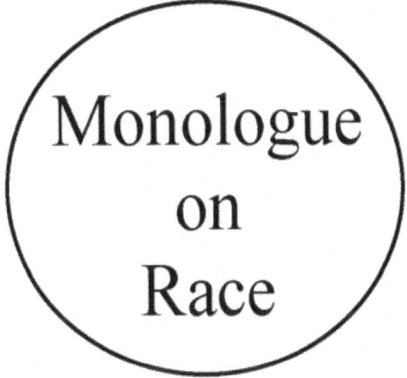

Monologue on Race

A Pump Primer for Afrodescendant Thought

Brooks B. Robinson

©**BlackEconomics.org**
Seattle, Washington
May 2013

Dedication

To our Afrodescendant ancestors who see the future and
await our rise!

Table of Contents

Prologue

What are the existential questions concerning race in America—specifically the United States (US)? Everywhere we turn there are discussions of race. The "N" word pops up, and then it is diffused with an apology. You walk down the street and see a Black male with a White female or vice-versa, and you are perplexed that irritation surfaces at the site. You hear about the high rate of prison incarceration of Black males. You read about the high rate of out-of-wedlock child births and the high rate of Black abortions. Most importantly, you ride through the Black ghettos of our major cities and see the scourge of poverty, and then you go to the movies, watch TV, or view the Internet and see the wealth that exists in mainly White suburbs.

In the 1960s, the 1970s, and possibly the 1980s there was a strong thread of unity among Afrodescendants. There were Black men and women speaking up and out about conditions in Black communities with expressions of hope that we could counteract our discomfort in America with a unified effort. Then came the 1990s, the breakout of the information technology (new) economy, the blow up of Hip-Hop culture, the explosion of sports, and one could begin to visually see the snapping of that thread as the "haves" versus "have nots" divide began to transform the thinking of Black America.

Many Blacks, especially those that considered themselves middle-class-and-above, unified themselves with the US after 9/11. We became one with the US against the world. Many of us benefitted from the economic expansion that began in 2002 and that extended to the Great Recession that took hold in 2007. However, the dividing line soon became evidently clear between those who had successfully climbed the ladder of economic success versus those who could not hang because they lost all or nearly all that they had through foreclosures and bankruptcies during 2008-2012.

Some argue that, as we move ever forward through the second decade of the 21st century, Afrodescendants have become so fragmented that there are no issues in America today on which all Blacks agree. They argue that so-called wealthy Blacks are aligned with wealthy Whites; that Black gays and lesbians are aligned with White gays and lesbians who advocate for same-sex marriage; that young Afrodescendants are aligned with young Whites who seek to make the world a more humane and environmentally safe place; and that poor Blacks are aligned with poor Whites in their efforts to squeeze from government coffers what they need to survive. If there is no unifying issue for Black America, then how can we talk about "solving the problems of Black America?"

At this critical juncture in history when the planners of civilization are on the verge of transforming the world into an international matrix where technology will redefine the meaning of man, woman, and human once and for all, it is important to stop and give 360-degree consideration to what this all means for Black Americans. What should we do? What should we think?

You will find answers to those two questions wherever you turn. But, really, what should you do and what should you think? What are YOUR answers? This monograph represents our efforts to stop and think systematically about the existential questions to which we referred. It represents our thinking. In the final analysis, what you do and what you think boils down to what you settle on in your own mind. The questions that we ask and answer are key questions that come to mind when we think about RACE in America. These thoughts can serve as a guide for Afrodescendants who want to take the time to think about key questions and make up their own minds about what they should do and what they should think. It is only a guide.

You may find that it is hard to find in your immediate circle the two or three who see the world as you do. Nevertheless, for your life to be meaningful, you must decide on your points of view, which will shape how you live your life. It is in that living that you ultimately come in touch with others who have a similar vision. If there are enough Afrodescendants who believe that we have been taken on a ride through a process of integration and separation, and believe that we should come together again as a people and chart our own destiny, then it may be possible that Black America will be saved for posterity. The ultimate existential question is, "How do we save Black America?" If we fail to answer this question correctly, then we may magically disappear from the American landscape.

What is Our Context?

In order to ensure that the reading of this monograph is meaningful, it is critical that we create a context from which to read. Here, "context" means prevailing conditions in which we now live. The context must be neither too narrow nor too broad, and it must be relevant to the questions at hand. Ultimately, this context must be such that the answers that we arrive at are consistent with the prospective reality in which we find ourselves. The following are a series of questions that we asked concerning our context as we set out to prepare this monograph.

Question: What can be ignored in fashioning this context?

Answer: We can ignore much of the history of Afrodescendants in America. While the nation may generally present a distorted version of this history, everyone knows the general history of the African American experience—brought from Africa to the Americas and over 400 years of slavery (physical and mental). However, it is important to remind readers regarding our tight relationship with Africa and concerning our national 1960s breakout. In fact, the latter point is critical because the 1960s represent the last time that Black Americans laid a strong claim to our African identity, and it was a period during which we made it unequivocally clear that we were willing to battle the police and military for our human and civil rights. We should hold these two 1960s developments close in hand.

Question: Where do we stand politically?

Answer: According to the pundits, we live in a "post-racial" America! We have an Afrodescendant president (African father and White mother), Barack Hussein Obama. We have more Black American representatives in the House of Representatives than ever before; we have no Black American senators. Nevertheless, economically, Black America continues to have great difficulty swinging the knife that cuts the pork or the proverbial pie in the nation's capital in our favor. The unemployment rate remains high and over 25% (over 10 million) Afrodescendants live in or near poverty. We have continued high levels of representation in state legislatures and on city councils, boards, and commissions. How can we have such high representation in political positions and continue to see such weak political and economic results for our people? The answer is that most Black American elected officials have little-to-no-power in wielding the pork or pie slicing knife. Why is this the case? Because Black constituencies are not sufficiently organized politically and economically to cause the powers that be to respect our politicians. We are in no position to make the power structure respond to our requests. In the 1960s, a different picture presented itself. Blacks demanded change (arguably the wrong type of change), and were able to make that change materialize. We were organized around a principle of give us what we request or else. Have we forgotten that history?

Question: Where do we stand socially/culturally?

Answer: Between a rock and a hard place! We have created and matured the most important cultural phenomena in the society, but we are not the ultimate beneficiaries of those creations. Think about Hip-Hop and other genres of music, professional sports, and the media. We are the outstanding performers in each of these cultural forms, which produce hundreds of billions of dollars in revenue. However, although our top performers are considered to be well-paid, the support players are paid poorly and the White controllers/owners of these industries are laughing all the way to the bank. We control little-to-no aspects of these industries. Yet, Black Americans are some of the most avid supporters of these industries. We love the music, we crave the sports, and we swoon and salivate as we watch our "stars" on television or in the movies. You say, "We have Black owners of a couple of National Basketball Association teams, we have BET, VH-1, and Oprah networks, and we have a few Black-owned radio stations." Our response is: "Yes we do. But do you know the ownership ratios? Who really owns what?

How much real power of ownership do Black Americans have? A close check of equity ownership of most of these enterprises will reflect that a White-based corporation has the controlling interest." Therefore, our decision-making control is miniscule. Consequently, we continue to be fed a diet of entertainment that glorifies "White beauty" and "Black compliance" with the status quo. Even within the institution (industry) that we own, the Black Church, although a message of prosperity is taught, Black gospel music fails to support and substantiate the message of prosperity because it is not laden with action lyrics that teach us to do for self. It turns out that Gospel Music mainly promotes messages of praise and that "God's Got It." Hip-Hop is not promoting a unified and systematic message of organizing to change the status quo. In other words, our social and cultural position is bankrupt.

Question: Where do we stand economically?

Answer: On very shaky ground! Despite our high unemployment rate, and over 10 million of us living in or near poverty, Afrodescendants earn over $1 trillion each year. This income, if considered on a joint basis, would make Black America one of the world's 20 richest nations according to income size. Yet we are directly responsible for only a miniscule portion of those earnings. That is, Black business employs less than 5% of the over 15 million Black men and women who are in the labor force. In fact, of the nearly 2 million Black businesses in the nation, less than 6% of them are large enough to hire employees. As importantly, we have estimated that in 2010, while the nation's governments spent over $750 billion meeting many of Black America's needs, Black America contributed less than $350 billion to the nation's coffers. It also bears mentioning that Black Americans have concentrated ourselves, work wise, in industries that are the most subject to modernization through computerization or robotization. Finally, we have shown very little concern for our poor brethren as reflected in the fact that Black America represents the most highly unequal group in the nation when it comes to income (high-income Blacks have a disproportionately large share of total Black income relative to poor Blacks). To put it simply, Afrodescendants have the potential to be a strong economic group within the United States; however, we must learn the lessons of self-love and self-support in order to cause that potential to materialize.

For completeness, we must acknowledge the economic condition of the Federal and State and Local governments that rule the land. They are in a near state of fiscal crisis. For the Federal government, while the nation's gross domestic product is in the $16 trillion range, gross Federal debt is nearing $17 trillion: $12 trillion held by the public and nearly $5 trillion held by the Federal government itself. It is true that this debt is partially offset by assets, including the fact that the Federal government owns nearly one-third of all land in the nation. (Wouldn't it be great if we could get access to some of this land so that we could learn to grow and develop independently?) For the State and Local governments, credit market liabilities are nearing the $3 trillion level. On a combined basis, Federal and State and Local governments are running deficits each year that far exceed $1 trillion. Therefore, Afrodescendants can expect very little assistance from governments than we are already receiving. Put bluntly, we should expect to see a diminution of support from all forms of government going forward as they seek to resolve their own fiscal crisis.

Question: Given this political, social/cultural, and economic context, and understanding that our most important issue in America is economic in nature, what are the relevant questions that we should ask and answer in our quest to become as independent as possible as quickly as possible?

Answer: The first question that we should ask and answer is: How can we reorganize ourselves in order to create a mindset similar to that which existed during the 1960s when we were able to create social and economic change? Of course, we should be more deliberate and scientific concerning the change that we seek to create, but we need to get back to a point where we are

9

organized and committed enough to change the status quo. Other important questions that we should seek answers to include:

- What is the key problem facing Afrodescendants?
- How do we learn to love ourselves and identify those who love us and are willing to do right by us?
- Which contemporary issues should we be concerned about without letting them distract us from our ultimate concern?
- Which institutions are most important to our success in revising the status quo and achieving our goals and objectives?
- Are more Black businesses critical to our success?
- Is more education a panacea for our growth and development?
- Where do Afrodescendants stand globally?
- What happens to us when we are successful at changing the current course of history?
- Conversely, we should ask, "What is likely to happen to Afrodescendants as we know ourselves today if we do not change the current course of history?"

What is the Key Problem Facing Afrodescendants?

When thinking about race in America, often we engage in wide-ranging discussions that touch on a variety of important issues. However, we often fail to focus on what we consider to be the key issue. In the final analysis, the most important problem that Afrodescendants face in America is economic in nature. Given sufficient time and resources, Afrodescendants can transform our condition in America and create a world for ourselves that is favorable in all respects. This section penetrates to the core problem.

Question: When we say that there are racial problems in the US, what do we mean?

Answer: Primarily, what we mean is that there is political, social, educational, and economic inequality between Afrodescendants and the broader American society—including relative relationships with Whites, Asians, Middle Easterners, and Hispanics.

Question: Should Black Americans expect to resolve this inequality given our history in the nation and our population size vis-à-vis the rest of the US?

Answer: Theoretically, the answer is "yes." The political and legal haranguing that has occurred in the US over the past 60 years has led Afrodescendants to believe that we have a right to erase the inequality and that such an outcome is a realistic expectation.

Question: Consistent with the Japanese adage that one should keep asking "why" until one is able to get to the heart of the matter, we ask "Why does the inequality exist?"

Answer: Inequality exists mainly due to lack of opportunity.

Question: What underlies the lack of opportunity?

Answer: Both prejudice in the larger society against Afrodescendants and the failure of Afrodescendants to create opportunities for ourselves contribute to this situation.

Question: Which of these opportunity barriers is most problematic?

Answer: In our estimation, our failure to create more opportunities for ourselves is the most problematic. First, Afrodescendants must decide the outcomes that we desire to achieve, and then determine which opportunities are required to achieve those outcomes. Second, we must decide what we can accomplish on our own to bring those opportunities and outcomes into reality. Our efforts to be successful in this regard might create such momentum that it forces the rest of the US population to acknowledge our ascension and to remove their open prejudices—or at a minimum reduce them somewhat—beyond that required by the law itself.

Question: Why do Afrodescendants have difficulty deciding the outcomes that we should seek to achieve.

Answer: The divide and conquer scheme has been relatively successful in preventing Afrodescendant unity on key issues. Afrodescendants who have been "successful" in achieving some extent of material well-being favor further integration and assimilation. On the other hand, many Afrodescendants who are in or near poverty have become convinced that prospects for a favorable future are dim; therefore, for them, there is a sense of hopelessness and a desire to stiff-arm further integration and assimilation. But it is not as cut and dried as that. Many materially well-off Afrodescendants have concluded also that their advancement is limited by prejudice and they too might opt for less integration and assimilation. However, they may fear that they are better off with the devil that they know and, thus, may not pursue a situation that is unknown and uncertain— even if conditions might be better under a different arrangement.

Question: What causes Afrodescendants to fail to create more opportunities for ourselves?

Answer: Fear. Mainly fear of failure. In addition, lack of individual resources causes many Afrodescendants to be unable to engage in entrepreneurial activities at a level that would be sufficient to produce favorable outcomes for them and others. Most importantly, Afrodescendants fear that other

Afrodescendants will not come to their support.

Question: Why do these fears exist?

Answer: Our deepest sense concerning why these fears exist falls on religion. Afrodescendants have, for so very long, believed in a White God. One who, especially at the subconscious level, comes to the aid of Whites in times of trouble before he comes to the aid of Afrodescendants. He is a God who is other than Afrodescendant. This lack of uncategorical faith in God makes it impossible for Afrodescendants to believe that we have the power and support from our God that guarantees success. Without this subconscious faith in God and lack of guarantee of success, we become unmotivated to act on our own behalf. We feel alone in the Wilderness of North America at the mercy of an enemy who brought us here and who continues to manipulate our situation to his own advantage and not our own.

Question: How can these fears be addressed?

Answer: It is not sufficient for a few to overcome these fears. The "gospel" must be preached to the entire population if a sufficient and critical mass of Afrodescendants will begin to act on the power and motivation that is supplied by an unyielding belief in a God that is our own. A God that looks like us.

One that is guaranteed to answer our prayers. Once "all" Afrodescendants have faith in our God and, therefore, ourselves, and that faith and belief is able to marinate in our communities for a couple of generations, then Afrodescendants can begin to think positively and systematically concerning the world that we want to make to live in, and what is required to bring that life into reality. Then we will have the power and motivation to go forth in faith with resilience of heart and mind to bring that world into existence. We must find our God and create our world. Caution must be taken, however, because we must be certain to create a world that is based on principles that are God-centered; i.e., principles that are consistent with our God and all that he/she stands for.

Question: What type of "God" must Afrodescendants identify as our own?

Answer: One that comes to us—to our aid in times of trouble. He must be a new God or a reinvented God—not an old God that has failed to transform our lives during our 400-year sojourn in America. We need a God who comes when we want him and who is always on time.

Question: Is the "correct" God then the key problem that we face?

Answer: No!!! As indicated from the outset, lack of economic resources is the key problem. For example, if you have physical needs and desire a higher level of income, how do you obtain it? Either you can develop your own source of income by becoming an entrepreneur or you can obtain the education and training that will lead to a higher income position. To do both, you need economic resources. If you have poor health that can be improved through medicine, how do you obtain such medicine? You need economic resources. If you are perplexed by a certain set of issues or an academic subject, how do you obtain answers? You seek out education and training. How do you obtain them? You need economic resources. If you know that there are opportunities in a different location, how do you get to those opportunities? You relocate. How? It takes economic resources? If you want to change a law that is producing an adverse outcome for you and your community, what do you do? You lobby the legislative body. What does it take to conduct the lobbying process? It takes economic resources. If you want to overcome racial exclusion and join some White dominated social club, what does it normally take to do so? It takes economic resources. And, of course, if you want to help transform the Afrodescendant community and make it more economically independent, what does it take? It takes economic resources. So, the point is well taken. To solve all of Afrodescendant inequality issues in America, we need more economic resources.

Who Loves Black America?

Admittedly, many Afrodescendants are living fairly comfortable lives. Any American (White or Black) can call the names of several rich and famous Black Americans. In addition, there are many African Americans who do not live paycheck-to-paycheck. Nevertheless, any politician, economist, or sociologist will readily rattle off for you a crucial statistic: Over 25% of Afrodescendants live below or near poverty. That is, over 10 million of the 40-plus million Afrodescendants know firsthand what poverty means.

Admittedly, poverty in the US is a far cry from poverty in a less developed country. Statisticians in the nation's capital who track poverty argue that US poor enjoy many accoutrements of life: Cars, air conditioning, computers, televisions, dishwashers, mobile telephones, and washing machines and clothes dryers. They argue that US poverty is a very bearable state compared to poverty in the poor countries of Asia or Africa. Therefore, we have a situation where the "haves" are left to feel not so concerned about the "have nots." In fact, many Whites and Afrodescendants alike will contend that "it is no longer about race, but about class:" Those who have high incomes and wealth versus those who have little-to-no income and wealth.

If you are between these two worlds and seeking to be on the road to entering the world of the "haves," you can quickly forget about poor Afrodescendants. At bottom, it is a moral issue whether you concern yourself with your poor brethren. It boils down to whether you love or care about them. Yes, it is true, that "if you cannot do for self, then how can you do for others?"

However, let us assume that you can do for self. Morally, then, it is your duty to assist those who require your assistance. As an economic agent you may think otherwise, but let us assure you that, in the long run, societies that do not manage well their poor will find that the poor ultimately helps to relieve the "haves" of their wealth. Therefore, for your own well-being, it is likely to be in your best interest to express your "love" for your brethren in favorable ways.

Consequently, we use this section to analyze whether you "love" (truly love) your fellow Afrodescendants.

Question: Who really loves Afrodescendants?

Answer: We take as a fundamental requirement that any man or woman who says that they truly love Afrodescendants must really love themselves. In other words, to love Black Americans you must be among those who selected the Black doll in psychologist Kenneth Clark's doll study. If you do not love your black skin, kinky hair, flat nose, thick lips, and almond shaped eyes—that is, what you see when you look in the mirror— then you cannot love your brethren. Unfortunately, James Brown's 1960 cry "Say It Loud, I'm Black and I'm Proud" has faded from the airwaves and no one seems willing to issue that call repeatedly again. Given the media's proselytization of White beauty, one can easily fall into the trap of loving that which is White. Therefore, if you want to say that you love Afrodescendants, then you must love yourself—in all of your African glory.

Question: Do Black leaders love Black America?

Answer: Following up our previous response, a starting point for answering the question is to analyze Black leaders to determine whether they accentuate the non-African aspects of their appearance. It is simple. If a person spends time transforming their appearance to mimic Whiteness, then they cannot be a lover of Blackness and, therefore, do not love their fellow Black Americans.

Question: How can we tell whether Black leaders and others love Afrodescendants?

Answer: Beside their love of themselves and their Blackness, we can look at Black leaders' finances. If a Black person (leader or otherwise) really loves Black America, then they will not reflect massive personal wealth. It may not be necessary to "give all that you have to the poor and take up your cross and follow me;" however, true love for the poor will not permit one to hoard wealth when there are those in need. It makes sense to use one's talents to achieve high levels of income and wealth. However, seeing the massive need, it seems logical that those who have the capacity would only retain that which is required to sustain themselves in a "reasonable" lifestyle, and to use the remainder to help those who are in need. Consequently, if we find that Black Americans who claim to love their people hoard vast wealth for themselves, then they are failing to adequately express their love.

Question: Should those who have high incomes and vast wealth and say that they love Black America give their income and wealth to the poor?

Answer: The answer is simple: Yes they should! However, they should be wise in their giving. They should give in such a way that their giving has maximum effect. The well-known adage should be followed: "Give a man a fish and he eats for a day. Teach a man to fish and he eats for a lifetime." In other words, Blacks who have should express their love for Black America by taking the time to research and find mechanisms that are effective in helping raise up our people. Such operations with an extended track record should receive support because they can do most to help raise Black Americans out of poverty and the depths of hell in America.

Question: What is the most important goal of those who love Afrodescendants?

Answer: A central goal of those who love Afrodescendants is to continue loving themselves, which requires that they learn as much as possible about themselves and their heritage. This knowledge will enable them to come to comprehend the historical greatness that is associated with Blackness and Africaness. This knowledge, in turn, will enable them to recognize that Afrodescendants have never been treated fairly in the American context. They should learn that there is a cost to be paid by White America for her cruelty, thievery, hate, lies, and wars. It should motivate them to want to separate from those who must bear the burden of such atrocious evil. Therefore, the end-game for those who love Afrodescendants should be to enable Afrodescendants to become as independent as possible as quickly as possible so that we can begin to thrive independently as a people. Those who perform these acts will find that Afrodescendants will continue to rise as White America declines.

Question: Can one who loves Black America also love White America?

Answer: Absolutely not! But let us caveat this answer. Blackness and Whiteness goes beyond skin color. There are Blacks who are lily White. There are Whites who are pecan tan. What we are concerned with here is a Black versus a White mentality. Simply put, those who love Afrodescendants cannot be in concert with those lovers of Whiteness and the related White Supremacy concept. Black Americans have been damaged for so long by our exposure to and the imposition of White Supremacy that we have become sick just as White Supremacists have become sick. Therefore, we need to undergo treatment so that we can be cured. The best medicine for White Supremacy is to learn to love Blackness. We can only accomplish this outcome by being thoroughly exposed to Blackness in a Black enriched environment. If we fail to receive this curative treatment, then we will remain sick—especially if we remain in a White Supremacist environment. Therefore, we should do all that we can to become independent, learn to increasingly love our Blackness; to the extent possible, outside of a White Supremacist environment. Once we receive the cure and assess history, we are certain to want to have little-to-nothing to do with those conditioned in a White Supremacist environment. Therefore, one who really loves Black America cannot love White America—specifically any aspect of it that imposes White Supremacist principles.

Question: What will signal a lovely Black American Society?

Answer: A lovely Afrodescendant society is characterized by:

- Black individuals who truly love themselves.
- Black families that reflect true love for each member.
- Black communities that are educated about our past and potential future greatness.
- A Black economy that is sufficiently productive to nurture the children and elderly, to provide a livelihood

for adults, and to lay-by-in-store for future contingencies.

- Wise governance that ensures truth and justice such that our language can erase "jail" from our vocabulary because there is no need for one.

Which Institution is the Most Poised to Solve Afrodescendants' Problems?

Historically, two important institutions have played key roles in helping lift Afrodescendants in America: The Black church and educational institutions. This is an indisputable fact. Logically, you might select either of these two institutions as the one most poised to help solve Black America's problems. If you did, then you would be in error. Both of the aforementioned institutions have a great deal to offer in solving Afrodescendants most pressing problem, which is economic in nature. However, neither institution is most critical to raising Black America to the heights that we are destined to achieve. Below, we explore the institution that sits at the root of our future success and we delineate why the Black church and educational institutions remain helping institutions.

Question: What is the building block of society?

Answer: The family is the building block of society. Therefore, the family is the most important institution for Afrodescendants future success. Yes, it is true that 72% of Black infants are born out of wedlock. Yes, it is true that only about 50% of Black households are comprised of married partners. Yes, it is true that less than 50% of Black females between the age of 25 and 45 have been married. Yes, it is true that one out of three Black marrying age males are tied up in the criminal justice system. All of this is true. However, socially, psychologically, and economically, there is no simpler way to turn life around for Black children than to have them be born, grow, and emerge from a stable and whole family relationship. In fact, the quickest way to end poverty is to live in a household that has two working parents—not saying that two working parents is the most favorable environment for young children. Nevertheless, a family is the building block of society, and until Afrodescendants decide to begin forming solid families, we will have limited success in achieving our full potential.

Question: Why do Afrodescendants have such a poor record of forming solid families?

Answer: There are at least two major non-economic reasons why Black Americans have such difficulty forming and maintaining sound families. First and foremost, there is lack of self love. To the extent that one or both parties fail to love their Black selves, causes one or both parties to fail to love their produce—their children. A self-hater is among those who willingly departs from that which he or she has produced—his/her offspring. In addition, it is a self-hater who fails to see the importance of nurturing his own kind. One who breaks the security of a family opens that family up to the harsh winds of life. Those cold winds tear families apart and bring death to the happiness and love that resides within the warmth of a secure family.

Second, it takes a strong family to automatically produce another strong family. Strong families provide a context in which a married partner selects his/her mate. Not only that, but a loving and strong family is there when newlyweds and not-so newlyweds hit bumps in the road. If you are a husband and you decide to do something untoward to your wife or family, you'll think twice about doing it if you know that your wife's father, brothers, cousins, uncles, etc. will hunt you down and do something untoward to you. You may not think twice if your wife has no family to count on to rein you in. The reverse is also true for the wife. Consequently, we see that self-love, love of own kind, and a strong family are important keys that are required to create and sustain strong Black families. On the latter, it may appear that we are in the "chicken or the egg" conundrum. We need a strong family to build a strong family. However, if we don't have strong families, then how can we create them? The answer is, "we must start where we are." It can be done!

Question: What other important factors reduce prospects for building strong Afrodescendant families?

Answer: There are a variety of other important factors that prevent the development and maintenance of strong Black families, but they are generally linked to one source: The media. Those factors include materialism, educational mismatches, and a tendency to marry outside of the race. On materialism, the media plays a key role in shaping expectations concerning marriage. Black women and men watch too many movies and too much television that reflect "ideal" marriages; replete with the nice home, two cars in the garage, and children going to private school. Too many black men and women want to create this materialistic lifestyle for themselves when it may not be feasible to do so. Failing in this effort, the two parties find a reason to vacate the marriage.

On educational mismatches, there is long-standing concern that more Black women achieve academic success than Black men; therefore, an educated Black woman is a mismatch for an uneducated Black man. The reality is that many Africans who were brought to America lived in matriarchal societies. In Africa, even today, many of the most successful entrepreneurs are female. Therefore, strong and intelligent Black women should not be novel to us. Black men should not fear a strong and intelligent Black woman, but should love and cherish her. At the same time, there is no sin if certain Black males permit their more highly educated Black wives to be motivation for their own academic achievement. However, all in all, if two people love themselves and come together in holy matrimony, then there is no such thing as an educational mismatch.

On marrying outside of the race, better put, preoccupation with other races, it is true that about 30% of Black males with college degrees today marry outside of the race, while less than 10% of college educated Black females marry another race. This is a purely psychological issue that is media driven and that is linked to a lack of love of self. If a Black man or women cannot identify a partner to love within the confines of the Black community, then we must question their love for themselves and for their people. If we love ourselves and our people, then our goal and our love should be to extend ourselves and our wonderful heritage to the next generation, and we should not be persuaded to do otherwise by a media that is designed to channel our mind and resources to someone who is not of our own kind.

Question: Why is the Black Church only a helping institution?

Answer: The answer is multifaceted. First, if the family is not well-functioning, then there is a likelihood that all members of the family do not visit the church. If the family does not go to church, then how can it benefit from the church? This is not to say that all Black families should go to church.

Second, and hearkening back to the section on the key problem facing Black America, many churches continue to promote a god that does not know us. Until Black churches, or whatever we ultimately come to call beneficial Black religious institutions, promote the God that is our God, they serve as a distraction—not a help to the development of strong and wholesome Black families. Imagine this, a Black woman casting all of her cares on a White Jesus; and a Black woman who has a personal and intimate relationship with a White Jesus. It all seems like a setup for convincing the Black woman that she should have a White man solve her problems. We all know that the favored scenario is for the Black man (a Black God) to wake up and do the job.

Third, the Black church has, for too long, been designed around preachers who have taken advantage of the Black community—including playing a role in the destruction of Black families. Black preachers in Black churches must revise their relationship with the Black community if Black families are to become strong again.

Finally, we have studied the nature of contemporary Black gospel music and found it to be wanting. While preachers preach a message of wealth and prosperity, gospel music mainly promotes praise and worship and fails to thrust forth a powerful message of doing for self. This type of incongruity must be resolved before the Black church can play an impactful role in rebuilding strong Black families.

Question: Why are educational institutions only helping institutions?

Answer: For too long, education has played an outsized role in the American society—especially within Black American society. The educated have received great deference. In reality, it is the entrepreneur who has made the community move forward. Remember that "Those who can't teach." Why value the professor of finance if he is not rich. It seems to us that the man to value in the society is not the one who teaches finance, but the one who knows how to make finance work for him, who can create jobs with his skill in the finance industry, and who can finance required developments in the community. In fact, we should recognize that most jobs that need to be performed in society can be performed by students with a high school diploma—given the correct and sufficient practical or applied training. This is not to say that attending the university is a waste of time; only to say that it may be necessary to complete college to be given an opportunity to perform a certain job in the society. However, do not fool yourself into thinking that a high school graduate cannot be trained to perform your job successfully. Therefore, this outsized role of education has served to divide us—families in particular. We have already discussed the so-called educational mismatch above. In addition, siblings develop rivalries and permit educational differences to disrupt their relationships—thus weakening an important component of families. Given these disparaging outcomes, it is important to place education in its proper perspective, to value it properly, and to use it to build and sustain, and not tear down, strong Afrodescendant families.

Which Contemporary Issues Should Concern Us?

As we conduct this 360-degree monologue on race, we focus on core issues. That is, we must perform in-depth analyses of the fundamental issues that define race in America. However, we must simultaneously consider non-core, contemporary issues because they, too, shape the status quo and affect our point of departure and strategy for transforming our world into one in which we can be comfortable. In our opinion, the following are non-core, contemporary issues (in no particular order) that must be addressed: Unemployment, Media Image Issues, Gay/Lesbianism and Same Sex Marriage, Healthcare and Pharmaceuticals, Illegal Drugs, Incarceration, Guns, and the Militarization of America. Although we mention some of these issues in other sections of this monograph, we skim the surface of these issues below in order to ignite your thinking about them.

Question: Why is the Afrodescendant unemployment rate so high, and what should be done about it?

Answer: Numerous factors contribute to the current very high rate of Black unemployment in America. Generally, the factors that do not contribute much to this outcome that are often cited include education and experience. The reality is that the dearth of Afrodescendant education and training and experience does not fully explain Black unemployment rate. Most Black economists and many White economists contend that, to fully explain the Black unemployment rate, one must consider the existence of discrimination in hiring processes. To put it in simplest terms, consider that most jobs in the United States are controlled by non-Black-owned businesses, and that hiring officials have a tendency to hire people that look, talk, think, and act like them. On the other hand, they may hire someone that an existing employee recommends. Because that existing employee is likely to be non-Black and because that employee most likely recommends non-Black individuals to the hiring official, it stands to reason that Blacks are often excluded from the hiring process. Put even simpler, knowing the ravages of unemployment, does it not make sense that a hiring official and his support system would lean toward lifting like persons out of unemployment as opposed to non-like persons.

It is also true that the US is moving increasingly toward a more highly technological economy. Unfortunately, Black Americans are disproportionately underrepresented in STEM (science, technology, engineering, and mathematics) industries. Therefore, it is no surprise that Blacks fail to capture our share of employment in growing sectors of the economy. However, Black are often overrepresented in declining sectors of the economy. Putting two and two together leads us to the conclusion that Black unemployment rates continue to rise or remain high.

We will address this aspect of the question further in the section on "Aren't More Black Businesses the Key to Our Success?" However, let us consider that, although Afrodescendants lead the nation in the rate at which new businesses are formed, the businesses that come into existence are without the wherewithal to employ substantial portions of Black workers. If we fail to employ a substantial proportion of Black workers, why do we think that others will employ them? Capitalism is about doing for self. When we fail to do for ourselves, we are asking to be left out in the cold.

Question: How problematic are adverse stereotypical media images of Afrodescendants and how should they be addressed?

Answer: The media has become such a pervasive component of our lives that we just cannot get away from it: Television, radio, books, newspapers, magazines, the Internet, movies, and mobile communication networks. When these and other media sources reflect adverse stereotypical images of Afrodescendants, they contribute significantly to our marginalization in the American and global society. These adverse images contribute causally (in a complex way) to the production of the following Afrodescendant outcomes: Higher unemployment; poorer academic performance (the "stereotype threat"); a reduced receipt of healthcare services;

biased treatment in the criminal justice system; and a general stigmatization in the context of social interactions.

Given that the backbone of media operations is "audience," Afrodescendants should be more proactive in sterilizing the production of adverse stereotypical images by refusing to consume these images whenever and wherever possible. In addition, Black Americans must lobby media image producers to prevent the production of adverse images and to promote the development of balanced images. Much like *Brown vs. Board of Education of Topeka, Kansas*, where a case was built against the harmful effects of "separate but equal," Afrodescendants need to build an airtight legal case (notwithstanding first amendment rights—freedom of speech) concerning the harmful effects of adverse stereotypical media images on Afrodescendant social and economic outcomes.

Question: Are Afrodescendants' attitudes balanced on gay/lesbianism and same-sex marriage?

Answer: Everyone has their own opinion concerning the accuracy of polls. Therefore, we will not delve into what existing polls have to say about Afrodescendant opinions about gay/lesbianism and same-sex marriage. Suffice it to say that there are many in the Black community that are generally supportive of this lifestyle choice. We, on the other hand, want to be clear that we oppose such a choice. We do not take our stand based on religious tenets, but based on natural phenomena. A late Black leader, who we will not mention here, taught that, if one has a question about the appropriateness of certain behaviors, then one should examine creation. If one finds that such behavior is a naturally occurring phenomenon in creation, then one has justification for accepting such behavior. On the other hand, if it is uncommon or rare to find the behavior in creation, then one should probably reject the behavior.

At the same time, we reject gay/lesbianism and same-sex marriage on the grounds that such behavior is not naturally productive. From an economic perspective, one of the surest ways to ensure growth is to experience population increases. Therefore, if too many agents in an economy adopt gay/lesbianism and same-sex marriage as a lifestyle choice, then it is a certain method for ensuring that the population does not grow, which produces unwanted economic variability on the downside.

This is not to say that we should hate those who adopt the gay/lesbianism and same-sex marriage lifestyle choice. Hate is a dangerous disease. However, in our view, Afrodescendants should make every effort to prevent and deter the development of such lifestyles in our communities because they may detract from our drive toward economic independence.

Questions: Are Afrodescendant attitudes appropriate concerning the expansion of healthcare and the use of pharmaceuticals?

Answer: First, it is important to note that the Afrodescendant tradition is characterized, in part, by using naturally occurring substances in the environment to treat all manner of sicknesses and diseases. Remember that the ancient name for the area that is now Egypt on the African Continent was Kemet—the derivative of the word "chemistry." Therefore, as a people, we are not adverse to specialized healing processes. However, we do not fully comprehend the methods and processes by which our ancestors identified the healing properties of plants and herbs and their specialized uses. What we do know generally is that the use of medicines was quite precise, restricted, and governed by the doctors in our communities. Families knew general remedies. If an uncommon illness occurred, then the doctors would be consulted and they would administer special medicines. Therefore, the expanding practice in America of resorting to "medicine" for every little and large ailment seems alien. The most important medicines for our bodies are food, plants, and herbs. We should use them the way our ancestors did, and not rely on the use of chemicals that have horrific side-effects.

Second, we should recognize that upwards of 20% of the US economic output is derived from health and related services:

Consultations with doctors and dentists, hospital stays, clinic visits, pharmaceutical use, health insurance, etc. Managers of the economy have learned that they can create jobs and make the economy grow by drawing economic agents into the health services industry. For example, you have a minor ailment and you visit a doctor. The doctor prescribes a medicine to treat that illness, but violates the Hippocratic Oath to "first do no harm" because that medicine has side effects, which can cause tremendous harm. You are then forced to visit another doctor concerning the side effect. If you are not careful, you end up in a hospital, which is a perfect place to contract an infection, which may be antibiotic-resistant. Unfortunately, there are too many cases in America where the treatment of small illnesses mushrooms into a full-blown health crisis and death. As a less severe, yet problematic outcome, we should make every effort to avoid accepting drugs to treat minor illnesses, which turn into a lifetime of legal addiction. We must be careful not to become expendable in a health system that will use any and all opportunities for experimentation in order to discover the secret to life and its extension and grow the economy.

In our opinion, while Afrodescendants should seek the best possible healthcare for serious illnesses, we should also learn to do more for self with respect to healthcare. If you are obese, have high blood pressure, or high blood sugar levels, then perform research and use exercise and diet to treat these problems more so than pharmaceuticals to the extent possible. We are likely to find that our well-being is enhanced because we learn more about our bodies, we use natural methods for healing, and because we learn self-discipline. It is that know-how and self-discipline that can be used to turn other aspects of our lives around—including helping us to achieve greater economic independence.

Question: What is the appropriate Afrodescendant stance on the legalization of formerly illegal drugs?

Answer: This is a "no brainer." The answer is that we should oppose such action. Alcohol is a legal drug, but its legalization did not render it less harmful. In fact, alcohol's legalization made the drug more harmful because access to it was increased. In addition, just because access to the drug was legalized, which helped fill US Treasury coffers, that legalization did not prevent authorities from arresting consumers of the drug. In addition, use of the drug can render one out of control, which can cause one to commit crimes that can result in extended prison terms. Believe you us when we say that legalization of today's illegal drugs is likely to have an identical impact as did legalization of alcohol. The bottom line is that Afrodescendants cannot benefit from the legalization of illegal drugs, so we have no dog in the fight. Finally, drug legalization mainly involves marijuana, and not cocaine and heroin. We all know about the destructive effects of the latter two illegal drugs.

Question: What should Afrodescendants do about the high rate of incarceration of Afrodescendant males?

Answer: We should do all within our power to reduce the rate of incarceration of Black males. Current data show that the disparity between Black and White male incarcerations is lessening. However, there is tremendous room for further improvement. We all know that, at a minimum, Black male incarceration reduces the pool of eligible marrying-age males in our community; reduces the pool of college-bound Black males; increases prospects for homosexual activity outside of prison; increases gang violence; reduces our voting power; contributes to the spread of sexually transmitted diseases including AIDS in our communities; and generally destroys Black families. Logically, efforts to reduce Afrodescendant male incarceration will positively impact each of these ills.

We have just described the impact of incarceration; now let us turn to actions that might be taken to reduce incarceration. In the final analysis, the incarceration of most Black males can be traced back to an economic factor. Whether the incarceration results from drug sales or use, gang violence, theft, rape, etc., the individual could have avoided his encounter with the criminal justice system if he or his family had had sufficient economic and other resources. Therefore, if Afrodescendants can effectively address our economic ills, then we can simultaneously address Black entanglement with America's horrendous prison industrial complex. By lifting Black families out of poverty, we help ensure that young Black males improve their academic performance and avoid the types of behaviors that ultimately result in a prison sentence. We concluded at the outset of this monograph that our primary problem was economic in nature. Importantly, successful economic development will, in turn, prevent Afrodescendant female incarceration from accelerating; it has been on the rise lately.

Question: What should be Afrodescendants' position on guns?

Answer: Unfortunately, too many Afrodescendant households are with and without guns. By this we mean, too many Black Americans are involved in the illegal possession of guns, which are intended for and are ultimately used for criminal purposes. In our view, this should cease. On the other hand, there are too many Afrodescendant households that are without guns and, thereby, are without any means of protection in the event of a crisis. This, too, should cease. Consider the constitutional right

41

(second amendment) to bear arms. In fact, the absence of arms in a household represents a failure to exercise full citizenship rights. In the interest of being prepared for any eventuality, more Afrodescendant households should acquire arms legally, and should train in order to be able to use them effectively.

Let us be clear. We do not advocate the use of weapons to cut short human life except in those instances when other humans exhibit unwarranted violent behavior against Afrodescendant life. In such cases, Afrodescendants would be foolish to fail to defend ourselves and seek to preserve our lives and our general well-being.

Question: Should Afrodescendants increase our participation in the US military?

Answer: It is common knowledge that America's preoccupation with fighting the global war on terrorism produced a dramatic increase in the nation's military spending. Even with recent efforts to plan military cutbacks, there remain many potential opportunities. However, there are moral, life, and economic components to this question. From a moral perspective, it appears problematic for Afrodescendants to participate in a military process that involves taking the lives and destroying the infrastructure of black, brown, red, and yellow people of the world. What have the latter done to harm us? This picture is

42

particularly sharp as the US begins to expand its role in Africa.

In terms of life itself, it is increasingly the case that loss of life in the US military occurs at a much lower rate than in past wars. This is attributable to the type of wars that are being fought and to the technology that is used to fight these wars. That is not to say that dramatic injuries do not occur. However, given the correct aptitude, it is possible to assume roles in the military that will not involve placing one's life on the line and the potential for injury is reduced substantially. Given these circumstances, one can build an argument for joining the US military.

From an economic perspective, there are many obvious benefits from joining the military. Individuals with any type of military service, *ceteris paribus*, are likely to have improved life economic outcomes compared with individuals who have no military service. In today's technological military, one can gain a skill(s) that can lead directly to a job upon departing the military under robust economic conditions. (Recent veterans have had less than optimal outcomes due to the slow economy.) In addition, the military offers subsidized educational opportunities; subsidized home loans; and subsidized health insurance benefits. Importantly, the leadership in the military is such that members may benefit from the cultural capital that resides there, which includes emphasis on a high moral code and high saving and investment. Finally, there is something positive to be said for the lifetime fraternity that veterans enjoy when they encounter each other in all walks of life.

In sum, while there are reasons to think more than twice about joining the military, there are numerous reasons to put on a uniform and defend the nation. In our view, if one can be selective about the positions that one takes while a member of the military and can avoid military contact with our people from around the world, then the benefits outweigh the drawbacks. It is important to keep in mind that veterans bring valuable lessons back to the Black community that can help defend and preserve it. This becomes all the more important as Afrodescendants seek to achieve increasing levels of economic independence.

Aren't More Black Businesses the Key to Our Success?

We stated at the outset that Afrodescendants' key problem is economic in nature. Willy-nilly, more Black businesses should help address this key problem, which is economic in nature. How many businesses do Afrodescendants operate? How large are these businesses? How many workers do they employ? To what extent do these businesses impact Black economic conditions? Would an increase in Black businesses automatically produce an immediate and significant improvement in Black economic conditions? Answers to these questions move us closer to understanding the road that we must travel in order to create an economically independent Black America. We make an effort to provide these and other answers below.

Question: How many Afrodescendant businesses exist?

Answer: The most recently available statistics on the number of Black/African American businesses in the United States are from the US Census Bureau and are for 2007. (The data discussed herein will be collected again for 2012 during 2013 and are likely to be available for analysis during 2014.) The data show that, in 2007, there were 1.9 million Black businesses, which reflected $136.7 billion in gross receipts. It is important to keep in mind that businesses are classified by ownership based on equity ownership. In other words, as long as a Black American or a group of Black Americans held 51% ownership of a firm, then that business was classified as being owned by a Black American(s). Relatedly, we must remember that some "Black" businesses are organized as such with non-Black partners in order to increase access to certain types (mainly government) of business contracts. Realize that if a non-Black helps to organize a "Black" business by supplying a Black representative with the resources to acquire 51% ownership, then we should not expect that "Black" business to operate in the best interest of Black Americans.

Question: How large are these businesses?

Answer: The Census Bureau reports that, in 2007, only about 5.6% of all existing Black businesses were large enough to have employees (there were about 106.6 thousand such businesses). These businesses had $97.1 billion in gross receipts and an annual payroll of about $23 billion. Notably, in 1969, before desegregation/integration was in full swing, almost 30% of all black businesses were large enough to have employees. That ratio has fallen steadily over the years as it has become increasingly difficult for Black businesses to grow to a size that permits the acquisition of employees. Importantly, the data show that only 14,329 Black businesses had receipts that exceeded $1 million.

Question: How many workers do these businesses employ?

Answer: Census Bureau data reveal that for all Black firms with employees, 909,552 employees were included on the payroll in March of 2007.

Question: How do these businesses impact Black America's economic well-being?

Answer: In most respects, these Black firms play a very small role in the Black American economy. Specifically, in 2007, the Black labor force was 17.5 million; therefore, with about one million employees, Black businesses accounted for about 5% of total Black employment—assuming that Black businesses hired mainly Black employees. In fact, this may not be true. On the income side of the equation, as noted above, Black firms with employees had a payroll of about $23 billion. This income to Black workers accounts for less than 3% of Black America's total income in 2007, which amounted to $800-to-$900 billion. Therefore, from both employment and income perspectives, Black business impacts the Black economy in a very small way and, therefore, has a marginal impact on Black economic well-being.

This outcome results from the fact that Black businesses are mainly small operations, which have few upstream or downstream linkages in the Black economy. Consequently, the money that flows through these firms may come from the Black community, but it flows right out of that community because operators must direct the flow to suppliers and auxiliary firms that support business operations that are typically non-Black. When the money does not turn over multiple times in the Black community there is little opportunity for other Black firms to rise up and grow; thereby, not generally enhancing economic well-being.

Question: Would an increase in Afrodescendant businesses produce an automatic and significant improvement in economic outcomes for Black America?

Answer: An increase in Black businesses could have a significant impact on Black economic outcomes if those businesses were the result of sufficient planning and coordination. As described above, if new Black businesses filled upstream and downstream gaps relative to current Black businesses, then more resources would remain within the Black community, which would facilitate growth and an immediate and significant improvement in Black economic outcomes. A problem, in part, is that it may not be profitable to establish such upstream or downstream firms due to economies of scale. For example, if an existing Black business is a shoe retail establishment, it is probably not profitable to establish an upstream shoe manufacturing firm just to supply that establishment. However, if sufficient planning and coordination could occur across the nation, it would certainly be profitable to develop a Black shoe manufacturing operation to supply Black shoe retail establishments across the country. As a side benefit, a Black firm could be established to transport the shoes to retail establishments across the nation. Hence, without sufficient planning and coordination, it is difficult to envision that additional Black businesses can lead immediately to a substantial improvement in Black economic outcomes.

Question: What critical factors must be in place so that an increase in the number of Afrodescendant businesses will have a strong impact on Black America's economic outcomes?

Answer: Besides the planning and coordination already discussed, there are two key factors that must be in place so that an increase in Black businesses can have a stronger impact on Black economic well-being: (1) financing (saving and investment); and (2) development of a supportive attitude by Black Americans toward Black businesses.

By nature, Black Americans are very creative people. We develop great ideas that are commercially viable. However, too often the financing necessary to convert ideas into products or services for sale escapes us. Often, White-owned banks will not accept Black business risk; therefore, the Black community suffers. Unfortunately, there are too few Black-owned banks. The Federal Reserve Board reports that there were just 26 Black-owned banks in the United States at the end of 2012. This is unbelievable, but true. That is, there was one Black-owned bank for every 1.5 million Black Americans. To solve this problem, we need to find a method for saving even more than we save today, and for translating that saving into investment through Black-owned financial institutions. Once we are able to develop more Black financial institutions, we will be able to create more viable Black businesses within a planned and coordinated context, which can help Black communities achieve solid economic growth. A question that we must ask is, "Why can't we develop more Black banks through one of the most resourceful institutions in our community—the Black church?"

Even in the 21st century, for whatever reasons, too many Black Americans suffer from the unfounded belief that "someone else's ice is colder." Too many Black businesses fail because Black Americans will not support/patronize the businesses. Sometimes, it is out of jealousy, suspicion, and because of price points. Often, however, it is simply the case that Blacks believe that the products or services being offered by a Black firm are not on par with the products and services offered by non-Black firms around the corner, downtown, or in the suburbs. As a solution to this problem, we must get over our jealousy and suspicion. We should bargain with the

Black firm concerning price. Finally, we should perform whatever research is required to prove that there are no real differences (materials, workmanship, and guarantees) between the products and services that Black and White firms offer for sale.

If Black America can overcome the finance and support hurdles, we will be well on the way to producing and patronizing Black business that can have a large and lasting impact on our overall economic well-being—making us a more economically independent people.

Isn't Education the Key to Our Success?

During 2011 and 2012, we interviewed four of the nation's top economists concerning the most important issue facing Black America in the decades ahead. Two of the four economists stated uncategorically that education was the most important issue facing Afrodescendants, and one of the four said that it was one of the two top issues that we face. Should these experts' responses be challenged? How is education the key to our successful rise? If, as a group, Afrodescendants matched White academic achievement, then would it help us to become increasingly independent? We address these questions and more below.

Question: What are the statistics on Afrodescendants' academic achievement and educational attainment?

Answer: This monograph is not designed to present a barrage of statistics. However, we refer readers to the National Center for Education Statistics' (NCES) 2005 National Assessment of Educational Progress (NAEP). The NAEP measured students at the 4th, 8th, and 12th grade levels to determine whether they reflected "basic," "proficient," or "advanced" reading and mathematical skills. Here, "proficient" means that students reflect a solid performance. It turns out that, on the reading front, while about 40% of Asian/Pacific Islanders and White 4th grade students performed at the proficient-or-above level, only about 13% of Black students did so. At the 8th grade level, 12% of Black students performed at the proficient-or-above level. For 12th graders, 16% of Black student read at the proficient-or-above level.

Considering math skills, the NAEP found that, while 55% of Asian/Pacific Island students and 47% of White students were at the proficient-or-above level, only 13% of Black 4th graders were at the proficient-or-above level. A similar pattern emerged at the 8th grade level. For 12th graders, 36% of Asian/Pacific Islanders and 29% of Whites were proficient or above, but only 6% of Blacks achieved that outcome.

Based on these results, we can conclude that Afrodescendants are lagging far behind Asian/Pacific Islanders and Whites in reading and mathematics at key junctures in the elementary and secondary school process. This is problematic because the reality is that one can train oneself to accomplish almost anything in the world of work if one can read and execute mathematical operations proficiently. The fact that so few Black students are able to reflect these skills means that we have trouble finding our way through higher levels of education and figuring out how to perform well in certain aspects of the work world.

However, presuming that academic institutions of higher learning stick to a standard in grading the performance of their graduates, we can rest assured that Blacks who complete bachelor's, master's, and doctoral degrees are as qualified as other graduates. The problem is that the rate of Black graduation with these degrees lags far behind that reflected within Asian/Pacific Islander and White populations. For example, NCES reports that for Afrodescendants who were 25-to-29 years of age in 2011, about 88% had completed high school and about 20% had completed a bachelor's degree. This compares with 94% of White 25-to-29 year olds with high school diplomas and 39% with bachelor's degrees. Asian/Pacific Islanders led the field with 95% completing high school and 57% completing college.

Question: How do we raise academic performance and educational attainment?

Answer: The economists experts mentioned at the outset of this section were clear on how to go about raising Afrodescendant academic performance and educational attainment. They set forth as a key identification of schools that were successful in raising academic performance and patterning more schools after the successful institutions. In addition, improving economic outcomes for Black households should also help improve educational outcomes; however, this is probably a "chicken versus the egg" conundrum. That is, it is likely that we must improve educational performance before we see broad improvement in economic outcomes for Blacks. Another important

54

factor that could raise academic performance, which was suggested by one of the expert economists, is to build stronger Black families. A dual-headed household can generally manage the economic and educational requirements of families better than a single-headed household. Of course, these comments fail to address how a lower incarceration rate of Black males, reduced drug abuse, less gang violence, and increased use of extended family relationships, etc. can enhance academic performance and educational attainment.

A factor that the experts did not highlight was the need to reraise the value of education in Black communities. Historical records are replete with cases during and after slavery where Blacks had such a thirst for knowledge and the ability to know that they taught themselves to read. They understood the value of education! They knew that if they could read, write, and cipher, then White charlatans could not so easily deprive them of their wealth and civil and human rights. Somehow, we have lost the important insight concerning the value of education. We must regain that spark that is symbolized by a true hunger and thirst for knowledge so that we can use knowledge to shape the type of world that we desire for ourselves.

Question: Is raising academic performance and educational attainment a necessary and sufficient condition for Afrodescendant

success   in   achieving   economic
independence?

Answer: Improved academic performance and
educational attainment definitely comprise
necessary conditions, but they are not
sufficient conditions for ensuring Blacks'
quest for economic independence. Educated
fools abound.   They have numerous
academic degrees, but they are involuntarily
unemployed or underemployed. In addition,
the types of education and training that
Afrodescendants attain matters.   We must
steer clear of fields that are on the drawing
board for extinction.   As important, we
should avoid industries that have the lowest
pay scales. In other words, while education
is critical to our success, what is more
important is knowledge of how to use the
knowledge gained to develop a plan that will
benefit us in our efforts to become
economically independent.

Which Global Factors Will Influence Black America's Drive toward Independence?

The world's nations are familiar with Afrodescendants' story of slavery in America, and with our slow rise toward equality. How many of these nations made direct and explicit efforts to come to our aid? How many were willing to challenge the US on its administration of human and civil rights? As African Americans extend our history with efforts to become more economically independent, how many nations do we expect to extend a helping hand? Below, we walk around the globe to answer the latter and other questions.

Question: Where does White Europe stand on Afrodescendant issues?

Answer: Currently, Europe is being traumatized by her continuing financial crisis, her declining White population, and the rise of immigrants—especially Muslim immigrants. In addition, she is battling with China and the other Asian power for influence in Africa and elsewhere around the globe. She is so bogged down with these problems that she has little time to look westward, except to invite the US to come to her rescue. Therefore, Black Americans should not expect White Europe to be of any benefit in the move forward. On the other hand, the rising immigrant populations in Europe, which are experiencing their own bouts of discrimination, may be expected to sympathize with Black Americans. Unfortunately, they are not in any position to offer much more than moral support.

Question: Where does Asia stand on Afrodescendant issues?

Answer: Asia is preoccupied with her economic rise. Key countries in Asia have their own unique attitude toward Afrodescendants. These attitudes are two-pronged. First, internationally, China challenges the US almost annually on the latter's treatment of Afrodescendants on human and civil rights issues. These political jabs from China are designed to place the US in a bad light globally on human rights issues as a tit-for-tat strategy because the US cites China often for human rights violations. However, Asian nations have no general policy for supporting Black American issues. Most Asian nations rely heavily on US economic and financial markets and they are not apt to ruffle American feathers by speaking out strongly on Black American issues.

Second, domestically, new arrivals from certain Asian nations (in particular, China, South Korea, India, and Pakistan) make it their business to exploit Afrodescendant communities. In fact, research shows that, at least in the case of South Korea, before coming to the US the population is exposed to the idea that Black American communities are great business targets. Therefore, it is not surprising that we find that, even today, descendants of many Asian nations are operating successful business establishments in Black communities—in the absence of successful Black businesses. Interestingly, many US residents, who are from Asian nations, practice the very strategies of unity (cliquishness), high saving and investment, and excluding other ethnicities from their social circles that Black Americans fail to practice. Due to these practices, many of these Asians are very successful, while over a quarter of Black Americans languish in poverty and despair.

Suffice it to say that, for all of the just-given reasons and more, Black Americans can look to Asian nations to provide assistance only when it is in their best interest to do so. Such an attitude is not likely to be very useful for us.

Question: Where do African nations stand on Afrodescendant issues?

Answer: The continent of Africa is very fragmented, and it is still being exploited and plundered mainly by Western and Asian economic powers. Although bright new leadership is arising in several African nations, there remains too much emphasis on rushing to modernity by borrowing from the Western world and from Asia. This means that much of Africa will remain in hock to the West and Asia for years to come. Consequently, African nations have limited resources to help support Black American issues. In addition, like many US residents who have arrived from Asia, many new US residents from Africa are sidestepping Black Americans on their way to higher incomes, greater wealth, and material success.

Question: Where do Middle Eastern nations stand on Afrodescendant issues?

Answer: There is an obvious link between many Middle Eastern nations and Afrodescendants in the US—the religion Islam. In fact, many Middle Eastern nations have supported Black American communities by helping to build mosques and Islamic centers in the US. Because Islam is the fastest growing religion in the US, it is not surprising to find these nations providing such support. However, that is generally the extent of their involvement in Black American issues. We should keep in mind that many Middle Eastern nations have strong military ties with the US, which is one of their most important suppliers of military arms. Therefore, we should not expect these nations to intercede vociferously with the US Government on Afrodescendants' behalf.

Question: Where does Latin America and the Caribbean stand on Afrodescendant issues?

Answer: South of the border, nations are awakening increasingly to a battle over inequality and injustice by residents of African descent and the remaining population. It turns out that people of African descent in these nations are looking to Afrodescendants in the US for assistance and guidance on how to navigate their struggle. Because some of these nations have not yet addressed thoroughly inequality, discrimination, and racism in their own country, Afrodescendants can hardly expect their support. However, Afrodescendants in the US should extend our support to people of African descent in Latin America and the Caribbean. The emphasis should be on helping these people to plot a long-term strategy that results in economic independence—not integration. We can show that integration, at least as promulgated in the US, is impotent in delivering general economic equality and a fair and just society.

Question: Can Afrodescendants look to international organizations to support our cause?

Answer: Theoretically, international organizations, particularly the United Nations, have rules and guidelines in place that could be leveraged to aid the Afrodescendant cause. However, the bureaucracy is overwhelming. Moreover, even if we were able to overcome all bureaucratic hurdles, the fact remains that the US has tremendous influence in all important international organizations. This means that it is unrealistic to expect to use key international organization to transform substantially the life of Afrodescendants in the US.

Question: Where does this leave us?

Answer: Generally speaking, Afrodescendants should not expect global factors to have a significant influence on our condition in the US. On the contrary, we should take it as a given that we are alone (except for our "God") in our struggle. As mentioned earlier in this monograph, in order to create change, we must plan to recreate the mindset that existed during the 1960s, when we were effective in moving our social agenda forward. As an accompanying strategy, we should do all that we can to support other people of African descent in the Americas. If we are effective in helping them engineer their own economic independence, then they may be able to turn around and come to our aid here in the US.

What Happens When We Succeed?

Those with limited vision often thrive on the struggle. They enjoy thinking and talking about, and working in, the struggle. They become so enthralled with the struggle that they fail to imagine what it means to succeed and move on to the freedom that defines success. Of course, "freedom means responsibility." Those with vision begin the struggle with specific thoughts in mind concerning what it means to achieve freedom—otherwise known as economic independence. In the context of race in America, the best solution for Afrodescendants and for the broader US population is economic independence for Black Americans. This section seeks to draw out the vision of what Afrodescendants will experience when economic independence is achieved.

Question: What are "economic independence" conditions?

Answer: For Afrodescendants, whether we concern ourselves with a separate territory (Shabazzland) or independent communities within the US, economic independence will be characterized by an unconstrained "voice" to shape the world in which we live. It means that there is a realistic potential to develop the framework and tools that can be used to construct the political, social, religious, educational, and economic life that we choose to live. In other words, we will have more than a physical voice to verbalize our aspirations, but the tangible wherewithal to bring our desired reality into existence. This does not mean that there are guarantees, only that there is the opportunity to use our full potential to work to create a desired world—with the operative term being "work." We will have the freedom to plan and work as diligently or as lackadaisically as we desire; keeping in mind that effort levels yield a commensurate product!

Question: What would the creation of Shabazzland mean?

Answer: In part, the creation of a separate, economically independent territory for Afrodescendants would mean that we have an opportunity to create a new Black nation. It would mean that we have a great deal of planning to do to determine how we would structure that nation and what we would produce in the nation. We would have to assess our human capital in making these decisions. Like other nations, we could make choices about producing our own food, clothing, and shelter and what to obtain from elsewhere. We could decide how to educate ourselves. We could determine the type of administrative, legal, and judicial systems that would manage our society. We could decide on the industries that we would like to grow and develop. We could develop our own currency and our own media. We could assess markets to determine what we produce for export. Importantly, we would have a place on the world stage: Determining the nations that we support and the nations that we oppose. We could decide who could and who could not have access to our territory. All of these decisions may seem daunting. However, when tackled systematically, given the expertise and experience that we have obtained from our sojourn in the US, we could certainly do a better job than the US in building a nation that satisfies our unique requirements.

Question: What if we are only able to establish economically independent areas within the US?

Answer: Under this arrangement, we would face many of the same tasks that are associated with developing a separate nation, but they would not be as far reaching. A large downside to this arrangement is that we could not escape bombardment by US systems, and would continue to be subject to US rules and laws. Due to physical proximity to the US economy, our economy would likely continue to be somewhat integrated with the US economy. Nevertheless, we would have more autonomy over our production and income than we have today. Obviously, we would not have the political, educational, and social autonomy that we would have in Shabazzland. Clearly, this arrangement would have to be viewed as an interim step toward full territorial autonomy.

Question: What would be the most important benefits of founding Shabazzland?

Answer: Besides those already noted, the most important benefit of establishing Shabazzland is the type of unity and security that comes with being part of a strong family unit. Some the best functioning societies are the most homogeneous (think Scandinavian nations). There is a special spirit that is derived from living in a nation in which everyone feels connected by kinship—in this case, the Afrodescendant kinship. In such a situation, you work hard and smart knowing that someone in the Afrodescendant family will benefit from your effort. You take pride in helping build a nation that you can call your own. Remember that in the US, because we have never been totally and completely accepted as a people, we could never cast our lot fully with the remainder of the melting pot. In Shabazzland, we would be one unified people.

Another very important benefit of establishing Shabazzland is the opportunity to preserve our unique culture, traditions, and racial phenotype for posterity. It would be great to know that our nation took the time to preserve African American history and culture for the future. In the US, it has always been a struggle to preserve our heritage as American events always eclipse African American events. Is it not true that, five, ten, 20 generations or more into the future, Afrodescendants should have the right to explore and know what it has meant to be an Afrodescendant in America since the 17th century in all respects? In other words, we can save much of Black America as it was known in the past and how it is known today.

What Happens if We Fail?

What happens in the US and in the world if Afrodescendants fail to take action on our own behalf to achieve greater economic independence? Simply put, the implications of such failure are severe. So many great opportunities evaporate if we fail to take a stand and stop the slide toward a world that is dominated by White Supremacist attitudes and that over emphasizes technology and materialism. Below, we attempt to delineate the results of such failure and we forecast other related and important outcomes in the world.

Question: What constitutes failure?

Answer: In our thinking, failure is not an option. Throughout history, Afrodescendants have found a way (with our "God") to address critical moral and ethical deviancies that became transparently clear in the US. Accordingly, our struggles helped ignite struggles for freedom, justice, and equality elsewhere in the world; especially in Africa, South Asia, and Latin America. Hence, the absence of the types of actions that we have prescribed seems oxymoronic. Our history in America chronicles our willingness to take action against all odds. We are a people of action!

Nevertheless, if we do not coalesce around a central theme—namely economics—and seek to assume greater control of our economic destiny, then this would constitute failure. As we noted at the outset of this monograph, all of our problems stem, in

68

whole or in part, from a lack of economic resources. Failure means that we fail to learn to save and invest more; to transform our support for Black businesses; to plan more effective integration of our businesses so that we benefit from upstream, downstream, and auxiliary businesses; and we fail to cycle wealth through our communities multiple times so that they grow. In addition, failure means that we do not exploit our full economic potential to establish more independent territories in the US, or in the ultimate case, to establish a completely independent territory (Shabazzland).

Question: Which conditions prevail under failure and what do we lose?

Answer: In addition to the conditions cited above, failure means that we fail to leverage the power that comes from unity that is derived from a homogeneous society. We fail to use that power to inure to ourselves a substantial degree of economic freedom/independence. We fail to produce opportunities to develop a society and shape an economy that is in our own image and likeness; i.e., that meets our unique needs and desires. Failure means that we lose the opportunity to have a voice in the world. Most importantly, we lose the opportunity to systematically preserve, on our own terms, our history, culture, traditions, and racial phenotype for generations to come. We lose Black America of the past, present, and future.

Question: What does the world lose if we fail?

Answer: Actually, the world is a BIG loser if we fail to achieve more economic independence. Such independence affords Afrodescendants greater freedom of expression vis-à-vis the inequality, injustice, and oppression that persist in the US. The world needs to know that these conditions persist and that no nation (including the US) is immune to criticism and to action to counteract these conditions when they exist. No question about it, Afrodescendants have existed alongside White Americans for over 400 years. Therefore, Black Americans, better than any other people in the world, have insights necessary to perform balanced analyses of US policies and actions and to challenge them when they violate human and civil rights in any way. And, if the US can be challenged, then certainly every other nation on earth can be challenged. In this way, Afrodescendants could construct a framework for creating greater freedom, justice, and equality around the globe. The world can hardly afford to have Afrodescendants fail to make this a reality.

Epilogue

This monograph was designed to facilitate thought about race in the US. We were not very concerned about characterizing race and racism; its nature is well-known. We focused mainly on how to think about the existential questions and issues that Afrodescendants face in the US because of our Blackness. As a nation of over 40 million African Americans within the US nation, do we not deserve our own space to build and grow; especially considering the fact that our opportunities are limited in the US? We concluded that limited opportunities are the result not only of White racists, but also of our inability to produce and take advantage of opportunities that we create for ourselves.

As we consider our future course of thought and action, we should ask: "Two and one-half generations ago (i.e., in the 1960s), did Black leadership bargain for the current outcomes when they decided that 'racial integration' was the road that we should follow?" Today in the US, many Afrodescendants are deprived, and we lag Whites and other ethnicities in most of the important social and economic indicators. It is difficult to fathom that past Black leadership expected the current set of outcomes. Today, we have the option of continuing to follow the "racial integration" course, which is likely to produce a further deterioration of outcomes. On the other hand, we can take the opportunity to break with past misguided judgment and learn to think and act independently in identifying solutions to our problems, which are mainly economic in nature.

In a world that is increasingly technological, what happens to a people who are often locked out of the STEM (science, technology, engineering, and mathematics) culture? If we are wise, then we will see the hand-writing on the wall, and develop a strategy for surviving and flourishing in an economy of our own. Such an economy would utilize our existing human capital, while giving us time to selectively gain mastery of the technology that we deem to be beneficial to us. We can think differently and design an economy that does not over emphasize materialism and technology, but is abundant in its provisions for the youth and elderly, while allowing adult workers to realize their full potential. As a result of this economy, we can preserve our dignity, our history, our culture, and our phenotype for posterity. At the same time, we can increase our economic well-being.

If we do not stop and begin to think seriously about where we are and where we are going, then we may find out too late in the process that we have been slowly phased and mixed out of existence. Then there will be no time to reverse course and develop a strategy for saving Black America. Consequently, we invite all Afrodescendants to begin a thought process for developing a new strategy for Black America's future. Our guiding principle must be that every action is designed to make our people increasingly and imminently economically independent. When we achieve this state of being, then we will have created an unstoppable force for good that will save our people and produce a grand future.

www.ingramcontent.com/pod-product-compliance
Lightning Source LLC
Chambersburg PA
CBHW070605290526
45790CB00002B/784